LETTERS HOME from ITALY

Lisa Halvorsen

BLACKBIRCH PRESS, INC.
WOODBRIDGE, CONNECTICUT

Published by Blackbirch Press, Inc.
260 Amity Road
Woodbridge, CT 06525

e-mail: staff@blackbirch.com
Web site: www.blackbirch.com

Printed in Singapore

10 9 8 7 6 5 4 3 2 1

Library of Congress Cataloging-in-Publication Data
Halvorsen, Lisa.
    Italy / by Lisa Halvorsen.
        p. cm.
—   (Letters home from . . .)
Includes index.
Summary: Describes some of the sights and experiences on a trip through Italy, including visits to Rome, Assisi, Lake Como, Milan, and Venice.
    ISBN 1-56711-416-4 (alk. paper)

  1. Italy—Juvenile literature. [Italy—Description and travel.] I. Title.
DG417 .H35 2000
945—dc21   00-009034

TABLE OF CONTENTS

Arrival in . . .

Rome

As our plane began its descent into Rome, I tried to catch a glimpse of the Colosseum and nearby ruins. I had been reading about them, and Rome's other attractions, in my guidebook. I couldn't wait to start exploring!

Rome is the capital of Italy, a boot-shaped country in southern Europe. Almost 58 million people live here. About 90% are Catholics. Italy is a peninsula surrounded by the Mediterranean Sea. About 75% of its 110,646 square miles are mountainous. The Alps, Europe's highest mountains, are found in the north. The Apennines mountains stretch from north to south. They form the backbone of the country.

Ancient Rome

According to legend, the ancient city of Rome was built by Romulus and Remus. They were twin sons of Mars, the god of war. An evil uncle tried to drown the boys in the Tiber River, which runs through present-day Rome. They were rescued by a wolf who raised them as her own. Many years later, Romulus built a city on Palantine, one of the Seven Hills of Rome. The city was named after him.

The manager of our hotel suggested we see ancient Rome first. So we hopped on the metro and headed to the Roman Forum. According to my guidebook, this was once the commercial, political, and religious center of ancient Rome.

Roman Forum

Vestal Virgins, Roman Forum

The Colosseum

View of Rome and Tiber River

Today, ruins of buildings, arches, and temples are all that are left of ancient Rome. I closed my eyes for a moment, and I could almost hear the shouts of a long-ago political rally. I especially liked the house of the Vestal Virgins. It once had 50 rooms and was attached to the Temple of Vesta. She was the goddess of fire.

The nearby Colosseum was originally called the Flavian Amphitheater. It reminded me of a huge sports stadium. Emperor Vespasian began building it in A.D. 72. It had 80 entrances, including 4 just for the emperor and his guests. It had 3 levels of seats with an awning along the top to protect spectators from the sun and rain. It could hold up to 50,000 people!

7

Ancient Rome

There must be at least a hundred stray cats living in the Colosseum. Our guide told us that they are protected by the government—just like an endangered species! Many years ago the Colosseum was used for wild animal fights and for contests between gladiators. The Christian martyrs who died while fighting here are buried in catacombs beneath the city.

We also visited the Pantheon. It was built in 27 B.C. by Marco Vipsanio Agrippa as a temple to all gods. Emperor Hadrian rebuilt it around A.D. 120. The entranceway has 16 pink-and-gray granite columns. Two Italian kings are buried inside.

The Pantheon

Piazza del Pantheon

Rome

This afternoon I learned that Rome is called the "eternal city." It's also the largest city in Italy. Its population is about 4 million.

We hired a guide to show us Rome's "modern" attractions. We started at the Spanish Steps. It was here, in the 1700s, that the most beautiful men and women in Italy waited, hoping to be chosen as artists' models. The steps link the butterfly-shaped Piazza di Spagna with Trinità dei Monti, a French church.

The most famous fountain in Rome is the Trevi Fountain, with its statue of Neptune. Our guide told us to face away from the fountain and throw a coin into the water. This means we will return to Rome some day. If you throw a second coin over your shoulder, you can make a wish. I tossed two coins over my shoulder.

The Spanish Steps

Trevi Fountain

9

Rome

We stopped for lunch at a sidewalk cafe. Like the Italians, we started with an antipasto (appetizer) of grilled vegetables. I also ordered gnocchi (small potato dumplings), cacciucco (fish stew), and for dessert, torta di ricotta (cheesecake). Everything was delicious! Our waiter told us that each of Italy's 20 regions has its own specialty dishes. And I thought pizza and pasta were Italy's main foods!

Sidewalk cafes

Basilica Square

St. Peter's Square

Did you know that there is a tiny country, called Vatican City, inside the city of Rome? It's where the Pope lives! It is home to St. Peter's Basilica, the world's largest church. That's where you can view the statue of the Pietà. It was carved out of marble by Michelangelo, a famous Italian artist, when he was only 25 years old.

Michelangelo also painted the ceiling of the Sistine Chapel while lying on his back. It took him 4 years. Other examples of his work can be found in the nearby Vatican museums, along with other great works of art. I really liked the elaborate tapestries and the ceiling paintings by artists Botticelli and Raphael.

Naples and Pompeii

Today we took the express train south to Naples. The guide on our city tour pointed out some of the magnificent cathedrals. We also explored the National Archaeological Museum. It contains some of the finest treasures in the world. It has coins, paintings, household items, and other artifacts from nearby Pompeii and Herculaneum. In A.D. 79 when Mt. Vesuvius erupted, these ancient cities were covered with a thick layer of hot ash and pumice stone. Thousands of people died. When archaeologists excavated the city more than 200 years ago, they found intact houses, temples, and shops. They even unearthed a bakery with bread still in the oven!

Lava-covered remains of a person, Pompeii

Naples

Temple of Athena

First Hera Temple with Second Hera Temple

I wish we could have visited Mount Etna. It is the highest and most active volcano in Europe. It is 10,991 feet high and is located on the island of Sicily off the "toe" of Italy. The country's other main island, Sardinia, is the second-largest island in the Mediterranean.

After visiting the ruins at Pompeii, we drove along the Amalfi Coast to Paestum. It was once a Greek city called Poseidonia. In 273 B.C., the Romans conquered it and renamed it Paestum. Today it's famous for its ruins, including 3 well-preserved 6th-century temples. One is named for Athena, the Greek goddess of wisdom. Two others are named for Hera, the wife of Zeus, an all-powerful Roman god.

Assisi

We traveled through central Italy to Assisi by train, passing many farms, olive groves, and vineyards. Our conductor told us that Italy's primary agricultural products are wine, olive oil, fruits, vegetables, beef, fish, and dairy. Italy's other main industries are tourism and manufacturing.

Assisi is located in the Abruzzi region. Millions of people make a pilgrimage to this walled city each year. Most come to view the crypt of St. Francis. Although born into a wealthy family, he gave up his riches for a life as a monk.

Assisi countryside

Assisi

Medieval castle

Religious procession

St. Francis is the founder of the Franciscan monastic order. He is buried in a huge 13th-century basilica on the Hill of Paradise. The basilica is really two churches, one built on top of the other. St. Francis is buried in the lower church.

Every October 4 a feast is held in his honor. Franciscan monks lead a solemn procession through the streets of the city. I bet you would get a good view from Rocca Maggiore. This medieval castle sits high on a hill overlooking the city.

Siena

From Assisi we took the bus to Siena, another walled medieval city. It is built on 3 hills and divided into 17 districts. Each district, known as a contrada, is represented by an animal, like a goose, eagle, or elephant. One district even has a dragon as its symbol!

Each year 10 districts are chosen to compete in the Corsa del Palio (Parade of the Banner). It is held twice a year on July 2 and August 16. First there's a procession with flag bearers, musicians, horses, and riders. Everyone dresses up in medieval costumes. The main event is a bareback horse race around the Piazza del Campo, a slanting, fan-shaped plaza. More than 40,000 spectators come to watch.

View of Siena

San Giovanni

San Giovanni

Narrow street in Siena

At the foot of the piazza is the Palazzo Pubblico, the town hall. A new friend told us it is the best example of Italian Gothic architecture in the country! Inside we saw some very old frescoes, which are painted on the walls. We also climbed to the top of the 335-foot-high bell tower.

From the balcony of our hotel we had a good view of San Giovanni. This black-and-white marble duomo (dome) is one of the most beautiful cathedrals in all of Italy. Inside, striped pillars of marble support a high ceiling. The ceiling is blue with gold stars. It almost looks like the night sky. An inlaid marble floor contains biblical scenes.

Florence

Today we went on a walking tour of Florence. Our guide told us that Florence is called the "cradle of the Renaissance". The Renaissance was a "re-birth" of art and culture that occurred in Europe in the 14th, 15th, and 16th centuries. Renaissance artists Michelangelo, Botticelli, and Titian all had strong ties to Florence. We saw some of their work in the Uffizi Gallery and the Galleria dell' Accademia. Florence is also the birthplace of world explorer, Amerigo Vespucci.

The Old Palace with the Uffizi Gallery

A fresco from the Uffizi Gallery

The Cathedral or Duomo of Florence

Roofs in Florence

The guide also took us to see Santa Maria del Fiore. It is the longest cathedral in the world. The front of the building, or façade, is made of pink, white, and green marble. The dome is covered with orange tiles. We climbed to the top of the dome. The views of the city were incredible! We were so high we could look out over the red-tiled rooftops of Florence. The dome is pretty impressive, too. It is huge! It is decorated with frescoes and stained glass windows.

Earlier today we strolled across the Ponte Vecchio. This bridge was built over the Arno River in 1345. It is lined with jewelry shops.

Originally, the shops were used by blacksmiths, tanners, and butchers. They dumped their waste into the river, causing quite a smell! A corridor above the shops was added later. This allowed the Medici family—rulers of Florence—to move about without having to come in contact with the public.

The Ponte Vecchio

Main street in Florence

Soccer players

Santa Croce

We also visited the Church of Santa Croce. This Gothic church contains the tombstones of Michelangelo, Machiavelli, and Galileo. It also contains an important collection of religious art.

I read in my guidebook that each year in late June, the Florentines hold a unique soccer match. All the players wear medieval costumes! This is to commemorate a match played in 1530. The game goes on for 3 days and ends with a fireworks display! But soccer is not played just in Florence. In fact, it is Italy's national pastime.

Genoa

We made a short detour to Pisa on our way to Genoa. This is where the famous leaning tower is found in the Campo dei Miracoli (Field of Miracles). It tilts because it was built on soft, wet ground.

Genoa is Italy's most important commercial port. It sits on the Ligurian coast, which is also called the Italian Riviera. Genoa is best known as the birthplace of Christopher Columbus.

Business square

Tower of Pisa

View of Genoa

Street in downtown Genoa

One of Genoa's most interesting churches is the Cathedral of San Lorenzo. It combines every style of architecture from Romanesque to Baroque! The outside is made of white marble and black slate. One of its most lavish chapels is dedicated to St. John the Baptist, the patron saint of the city.

We took a walk along Via Garibaldi, a street lined with palaces. The famous Flemish painter Van Dyck once owned one of these huge houses. But the best part of our tour was taking the cable car to the summit of Monte Righi. At the top, we examined one of the massive gates in the 17th-century city walls up close. The view of the city below was spectacular, too!

23

Milan

Milan is the commercial capital of Italy. It is also known for its fashion industry. Italy's second-largest city is home to the second-largest church in the world. This giant cathedral on the Piazza del Duomo looks like a big wedding cake! It is 515 feet long and has 135 marble spires and 2,245 marble statues and gargoyles. And that's just on the outside!

Piazza del Duomo

View of Milan

Flower stall

Galleria

We also peeked inside La Scala. It is the world's most famous opera house. Afterwards we went shopping for souvenirs in the Galleria, an area of shops and restaurants enclosed in a glass dome.

In the late 15th century Ludovico Sforza, the duke of Milan, hired an architect from Florence named Leonardo da Vinci to work on his home. While in Milan, da Vinci, who was also an artist, painted the famous Last Supper on the walls of the monastery of Santa Maria delle Grazie.

Lake Como/Northern Border

From Milan we traveled north to Lake Como. This wishbone-shaped lake is one of the most beautiful in Italy. With a maximum depth of 1,358 feet, it's also the deepest lake in Europe. At the northern end of the lake, we had a nice view of the Alps. This 750-mile-long range lies in Italy and 8 other countries.

We continued along Italy's northern border to Parco Nazionale dello Stelvio in the Dolomite Mountains. It's the largest of Italy's 7 national parks. While hiking, we spotted a couple of marmots and an eagle.

Dolomite Mountains

Como Lake village

On the way to Venice, our last stop, we ate lunch in the resort town of Cortina d'Ampezzo. This was the site of the 1956 Winter Olympics. You can ski here year round.

Venice was my favorite city in all of Italy. It is built on 117 small islands. It has 150 canals and more than 400 bridges! The main waterway is called Canale Grande or Grand Canal. From the Rialto Bridge we watched gondolas and vaporetti (water buses) carrying people and goods.

Rialto Bridge

The Port of Venice

Venice

Nearby, at the famous Rialto Markets, Venetians were buying seafood at the Pescheria (fish market) and produce at the Erberia (fruit and vegetable market) for their evening meals. Looking at all that food made me hungry!

We walked along Venice's narrow streets to Piazza San Marco. Some of the city's most magnificent sights, including the Basilica di San Marco and the Campanile (bell tower), are found on this square.

Marketplace

View of San Marco and Campanile

Grand Canal

Clock tower

The basilica was built in the 11th century. This is where St. Mark is buried. Four bronze horses stand guard over the main entrance. The interior is decorated with beautiful mosaics.

The clock tower in the square was built in the late 15th century. It displays the phases of the moon and the signs of the zodiac. Every hour, lifelike bronze figures strike the bell.

Venice

We also toured Doges' Palace, which once housed the offices of State. The Bridge of Sighs connects the palace to the old prison. It supposedly got its name from the sighs of the prisoners being taken to trial.

From the palace we hopped on a vaporetto for a ride to the island of Murano to tour the Glassworks Museum. Did you know that eyeglasses were invented in Venice in the 13th century? I liked watching the glassblowers make vases and other objects.

Gondolier, Grand Canal

Doges' Palace

Vaporetto in the Canal

I wish we could be here for Carnival. It starts 10 days before Lent. Everyone wears colorful costumes and beautiful face masks.

As we said "arrivederci" (good bye) to Italy, I couldn't help but wonder when I will return again. Although I learned a lot about the history, culture, and daily life of the Italians, there is so much more I want to see and do.

Glossary

Catacombs a series of vaults or galleries in an underground burial place.

Crypt a burial chamber.

Fresco the technique of painting with watercolors on wet plaster.

Gladiator a Roman, often a slave, who fought other men or animals.

Marmot a rodent with coarse hair and a bushy tail.

Martyrs persons who choose to suffer or die for their principles or beliefs.

Medieval relating to the Middle Ages, the period of European history between A.D. 476-1450.

Renaissance a period, which began in Italy, of great revival of art, literature, and learning in the 14th, 15th, and 16th centuries.

For More Information

Books

Allen, Derek. *Italy* (Country Fact Files). Chatham, NJ: Raintree/Steck Vaughn, 1996.

Clare, John D. (editor). *Italian Renaissance* (Living History). Orlando, FL: Gulliver Books, 1995.

Rice, Christopher and Melanie. *DK Discoveries: Pompeii: The Day a City Was Buried.* New York, NY: Dorling Kindersley, 1998.

Stein, Richard Conrad. *Rome* (Cities of the World). Danbury, CT: Children's Press, 1997.

Web Site

Web Gallery of Art

Look at European art from 1200 to 1700 and learn about the artists—www.gallery.euroweb.hu.

Index